IMPROVISED LOCK PICKS

IMPROVISED LOCK PICKS

(FORMERLY TITLED : POLICE GUIDE TO LOCK PICKING)

www.bigfontbooks.com

ISBN-10: 1-940849-61-6
ISBN-13: 978-1-940849-61-4

Contents

FOREWORD

From regular law enforcement to security guards - from gun shop owners to alarm installers - all are expected to know the answers to the general public's questions about physical security.

With all that has been published in the last few security conscious years most everyone knows the virtues of a dead-bolt latch versus a spring bolt latch; the vulnerability of a sliding arcadia door, casement windows, and exposed hinge pins; the need for security chains & peep holes on front doors, etc.

Most all people concerned are well advised and knowledgeable in most of these "standard" areas of physical security. However, the subject of "lock picking", "lock picks", and pick proof locks" affords a large grey area of confusion and misinformation.

Misled by TV detective & spy shows, where the hero or villain as the case may be is able to pick his way, usually with only one hand, through about any "locked in" or "locked out" situation and also by manufacturers seeking to promote their latest "pick proof cylinder", the average person is prone to consider "lock picking" as a standard modus operandi for any would be burglar.

The purpose of this book is to shed light on the subject of lock picking and better equip the reader to make the proper decisions concerning physical security. There will be those who will consider publishing this book as a contribution to the training of potential criminals. Those so naive may rest assured that any among us possessing larcenous intent already know this subject well, if lock picking happens to be a needed skill.

BASIC LOCK DESIGN

Before a general study of lock picking can be made the basics of lock design should be considered. Let us first think in terms of what a lock is and how it achieves its purpose. Basically, a lock is a latch intended on holding the object to which it is attached in a certain position. A simple gate latch is, by definition, a lock. It does not require a key, only the knowledge and dexterity to perform a simple movement. Fortunately, for the farmer, cattle and other farm animals do not normally possess this knowledge and dexterity. We say "normally possess" because- occasionally an animal will learn to manipulate or "pick" a gate or door open. In effect, this animal is a "lock picker", the pick being that part of their anatomy used to open the latch.

We are purposely boring you with this Aesop's fable to align our thinking about lock design and consequently lock picking methods.

Early lock design was hardly more than a simple latch operated by either a device (key) or knowledge (combination, secret keyway, etc.) possessed, hopefully, by only those with rightful access to the contents beyond.

But man, being a clever sort, was soon able to devise ways of opening these locks without a key. This, of course, prompted other "clever sorts" to design more "pick-resistant" devices. Most common designs required a device (key) to be inserted and rotated. Further refinements introduced special shaped keyholes, receiving only keys of similar profile.

Other refinements were internal structures known as "wards" that required matching cuts on the key before the key would turn after being inserted. This basic design is still prevalent today in low security locks as found in some luggage, cases, cupboards, cheap lock boxes, and padlocks. They, as a group, are known as "warded locks".

Little revolutionary design came about until the 1850's when Linus Yale, Sr. invented the now universally used pin tumbler lock. Until this time lock designers seemed to focus more attention to the ornate exterior than to the internal mechanism.

Yale's design was not as revolutionary as it was a mechanically sound adaption of earlier Egyptian design principles. It combined both high security and ease of manufacture. Ease of manufacture lends to mass production which yields relative low cost to the consumer. Until Yale's invention, high security locks were usually handmade by some locksmith at a much higher cost and even these reflected more attention to the exterior ornamentation than to the internal mechanism. This basic pin tumbler design is found today in millions of locks. Even some of the "pick-proof" designs are adaptions of this earlier design.

Economics are always a controlling factor where physical security is concerned. Economics affords us with material possessions. Sometimes for economic reasons, other people want to relieve us of those possessions. For economic reasons manufacturers provide us with devices to protect our possessions.

Lock manufacturers make locks for one basic reason - to make money for the owner or stockholders of the company. Fighting crime is nice but it is so much nicer to make money while doing it.

Lock making is now a highly competitive business which requires thousands if not millions of dollars of investment in mass production equipment and tooling. Lock product marketing is quick to capitalize on consumer attitudes and try to "get there first" with what will sell the best.

In today's security conscious market place we are being deluged with security products, many of questionable value. Other products, while useful, should have been "standard equipment" on our homes or buildings when we bought them new. The author is opposed to laws , permits, codes and other bureaucratic trappings; however, still believes that an informed buying public should demand that builders do better.

In the last few years this "security consciousness" has inspired manufacturers to produce or market "pick resistant" locks and cylinders. Most manufacturers are careful to avoid using the term "pick proof" because this is an absolute term and leaves them no way out should someone succeed in picking their lock. We will take a closer look at some of these pick resistant" locks later in this book.

As a closing thought on basic lock design we should examine the purpose of a lock as part of a physical security system. No lock, even the "high security" versions will absolutely prevent access to the secure area. A lock can only provide two basic functions: make the potential intruder expend time and make noise. The more of either or both, the better the lock. Also, remember that a security system, like a chain, is no better than the weakest link.

LOCK PICKING

Definition of "Lock picking" - The means of opening a lock mechanism by the intrusion of a tool or mechanical device, other than the normal operating key. This tool can be as simple as a bent paper clip or an expensive pick set or pick gun.

Why Locks Can Be Picked - A lock mechanism becomes vulnerable to picking for two basic reasons: design shortcomings and manufacturing shortcomings. Both of these flaws are directly related to the selling price of the locking device. The design flaw allows a pick, wire, pick key, paper clip, hair pin, knife blade, etc. to be inserted into the keyway in such a manner as to reach and operate the mechanism. Manufacturing shortcomings are found in loose tolerances in the manufacturing process. A tolerance is a necessary sloppiness that is found even in the most expensive of machine products. For example: an .250 in. diameter hole will seldom if ever be exactly .250. The closer to perfection the higher the cost. Therefore, whether in a lock or an automobile, a compromise must be arrived at the engineering level. Basically, an engineer will strive to make the part as cheap as possible and as precise as possible. In lock design a third requirement becomes more important than in some other products and that is strength and durability.

The vulnerability of tolerance is usually found in areas such as pin diameters versus pin hole diameters and a row of pin holes deviating from a straight line. Tolerances allow shims to be inserted in the small space necessary between moving parts. Tolerances allow a combination lock to reveal its inner secrets to a skilled manipulator. Tolerances, like the air around us are ever present in any machined product. They cannot be eliminated, only minimized which directly affects the cost of the part. By this time, if you are still reading this book, you may have come to the conclusion that lock picking is a highly skilled technical complicated operation requiring mechanical savoy and dexterity beyond the majority of Joe Blows. If you have, then you are on the purpose of this book which is to show how difficult picking really is and why the average four thumbed, knuckle dragging, larcenous klutz does well to open a lock with the proper key let alone pick it. A good pick man is about as rare as a good counterfeit plate engraver.

METHODS OF PICKING

Simple Warded Locks - These are typically found in cheaper padlocks, file boxes, luggage, etc. The keys are usually stamped from flat steel and nickel plated. Higher quality warded locks sometimes use corrugated keys in an effort to provide better security and also make the key stronger. Three such padlocks are shown in Figure 1. Their respective keys are also shown. A closer look will reveal that each key has the ward cuts in a slightly different position.

Internally, the mechanism is basically as shown in Figure 2. In this illustration we see a flat, hairpin type spring that latches into notches in the shackle. Only a portion, usually the tip of the key actuates the spring latch. Turning the key spreads the spring latch apart, releasing the shackle. It is easy to see that a pick for this simple design would only have to be a paper clip or wire with a small "L" bent on one end.

A pick key shaped as shown in Figure 3 would also operate any such lock whose keyway would accept it. This is simply a key with all the ward cuts opened up, leaving only the portion on the tip that is necessary to operate the latch spring.

Manufacturers, in an effort to improve the security of this basic locking mechanism, have now added another spring latch with a ward between them. This design complicates efforts to pick it with a bent wire as previously done. How- ever, a double headed pick key will do the job. Such a key is shown in Figure 4. This key will operate all three locks pictured in Figure 1. Manufactured pick key sets such as shown in Figure 5 are commercially available to locksmiths and law enforcement agencies.

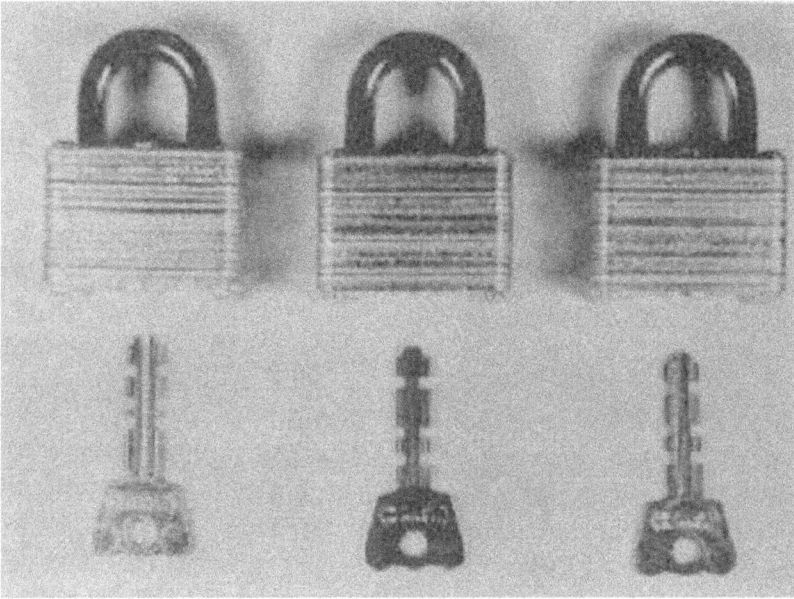

Fig 1

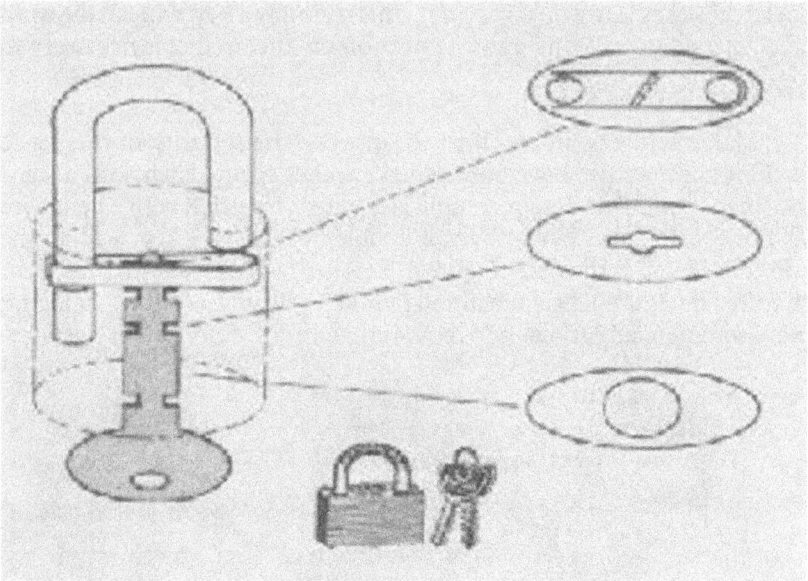

Fig 2

Fig 3

Pin Tumbler Locks - This is by far the most common type lock mechanism found today and is the type which applies to the picking most commonly referred to in articles on security, and distorted on TV.

To understand picking this lock we must be familiar, to a limited degree, with its mechanism. Manufacturers have dozens of versions of this mechanism yet they are all basically the same mechanically. The drawings in Figures 5 and 6, and also the picture in Figure 7, show a basic mechanism. While they can have more or less, the average pin tumbler lock has five sets of tumbler pins consisting of a spring, top pin, and bottom pin. The springs and top pins are usually the same length. The bottom pins vary in length to match the depth of the cuts in the key. When a key is inserted into the lock plug this set of pins is raised, compressing the spring. If the proper key has been inserted the bottom pins are all raised until they are flush with the diameter of the plug. This is also known as the shear line. At this point the plug is free to turn and release or activate whatever mechanism it is attached to.

To pick this mechanism we must somehow raise these pins or manipulate them so as to allow the plug to turn. Most methods of picking this lock rely on the presence of tolerances as we discussed earlier. In observing the picture and drawings previously mentioned, the tumbler pin holes seem to be the same diameter and also, in a straight line. They are supposed to be and the manufacturer has made a noble effort to do this within the limitations of the selling price of the lock. However, if we were to measure each part of the lock pictured in Figure 8 with a precision measuring device, we would find that the diameters of both the pins and holes may vary slightly from pin to pin and from hole to hole. Also, the holes, instead of being in a perfectly straight line will vary slightly from side to side. This variation may be only a fraction of a thousandth of an inch but is enough to aid picking.

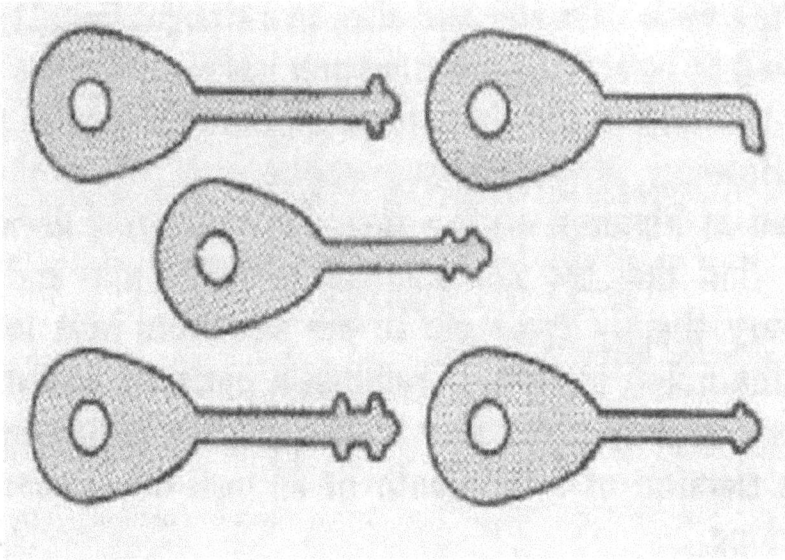

Fig 4

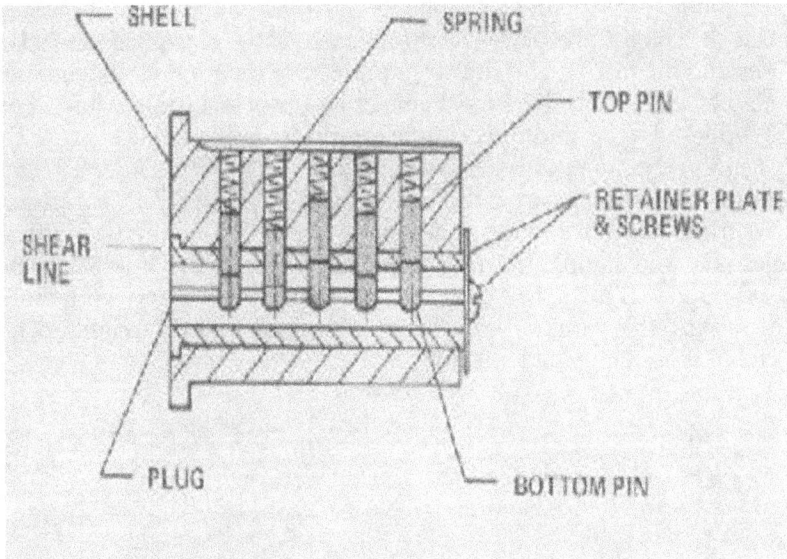

Fig 5

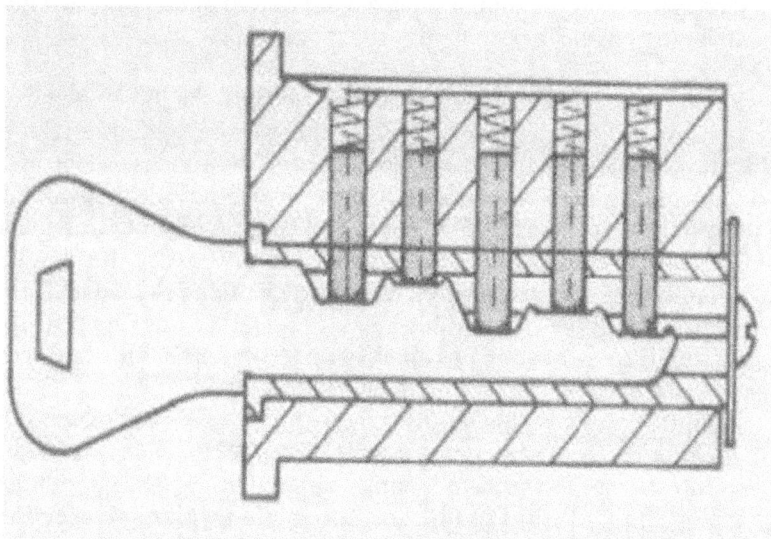

Fig 6.

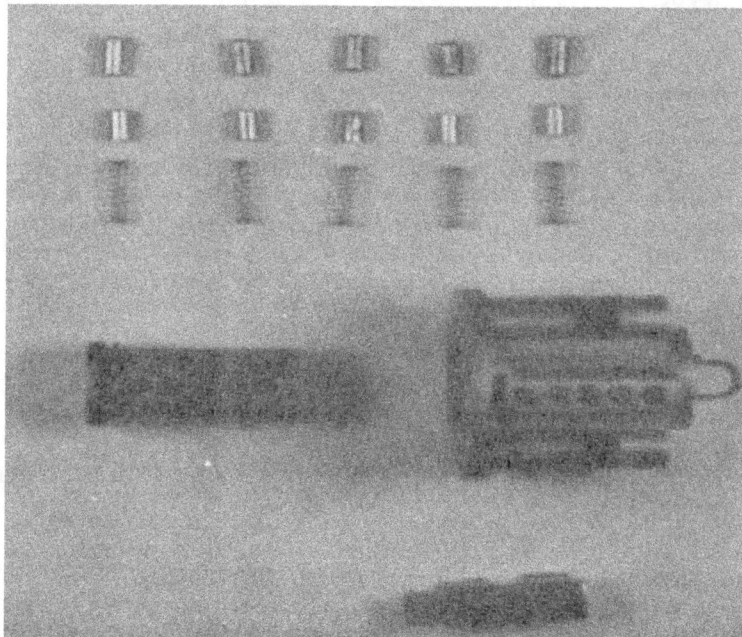

Fig 7.

At this time the plug may give slightly in the direction that torque is being applied. This operation is repeated on the remaining pins, at which time the plug will be free to turn.

Raking is another method of picking, perhaps the most often used because less skill is required as the lock opens more by chance than by skill. A rake tool has two or three up and down areas and is used in an in and out and up and down motion. The shape together with the random motion may at some unknown moment raise the bottom pins to the right level. If a small torque is being applied at this instant the plug will turn. Another form of raking involves using a diamond shaped tool. This tool is inserted all the way into the keyway and jerked out very fast. This motion tends to throw the pins apart because of inertia. This opens the area at the shear line permitting the plug to turn.

Yet another form of opening a pin tumbler lock, while not picking in the purest sense, is with a tool known as a snap pick. The mechanical principle behind this method is the same as used with more expensive pick guns. A snap pick is shown in Figure 9. It is kind of an overgrown safety pin looking device made from spring steel. The "pick" portion of this tool is inserted into the keyway and held so that it just touches the bottom pins (all of them at the same time). The thumb presses the bail down then releases it. The bail snaps back hitting the pick. This imparts a sharp rap to the bottom pins. The bottom pins, remaining relatively stationary, transfer this force to the top pins which move upward, compressing the spring. This results in the top and bottom pins being apart at the shear line for ever so small a period of time. If at this time a slight turning force is being applied, the plug will turn.

Any who has played pool can appreciate this method. For example: the number one and nine ball are just touching. You strike the nine ball with the cue ball. The nine ball remains stationary while the number one ball moves. This very same principle applies when using a pick gun which we will now discuss.

Pick Guns - Perhaps the most misunderstood tool to the uninitiated is the lock pick gun as we choose to call it. Over the years there have existed several versions of this basic tool. The most popular one is pictured in Figure 10. A Taiwan version is shown in Figure 11. Clever those Chinese.

On the outside of the American made version of this tool is stamped the Patent Number 1997362. We are amused at the thought of the Chinese ordering a copy of this patent from the U. S. Patent Office as we did. It just so happens that Patent Number 1997362 was assigned on April 9,

1935 to E. A. Davis for a two compartment water bucket!!!!!!! Seems you just can't trust **anyone anymore**.

One advertisement for a pick gun tool cautions the reader that complete identification must be provided for ordering this tool which, in the wrong hands, could virtually cause a "crime wave". This is pure bologna! These tools require as much as much, if not more skill than conventional pick- ing and most agree that a skilled picker with a hand pick is better equipped than someone with little or no skills armed with a pick gun. The only application where this tool has an advantage is on cylinders equipped with mushroom pins or other similar pin design which makes conventional picking a lot more difficult, sometimes impossible. Mushroon pins are discussed in a later portion of this book.

The picture in Figure 11 shows the pick gun being used. It is a two handed operation with one hand using the conventional torsion wrench to impart a slight turning force. The drawing in Figure 12 better shows how the pick gun works. Internally, the pick gun is akin to a double action revolver. Squeezing the long "trigger" forces an internal "hammer" to compress an adjustable spring. Near full compression, the sear releases the hammer for its forward travel at the end of which it hits the pick holder. This causes the pick to travel upward in a snapping motion. If properly held in the keyway it will impart the same motion to the tumbler pins as did the snap pick. The drawing in Figure 14 better shows just how this happens.

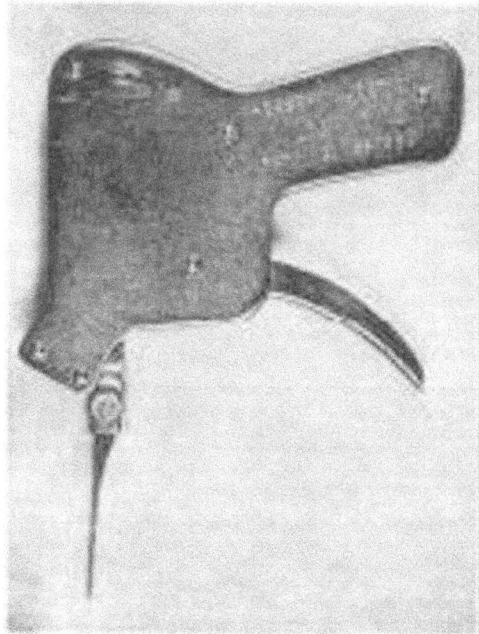

Fig 8

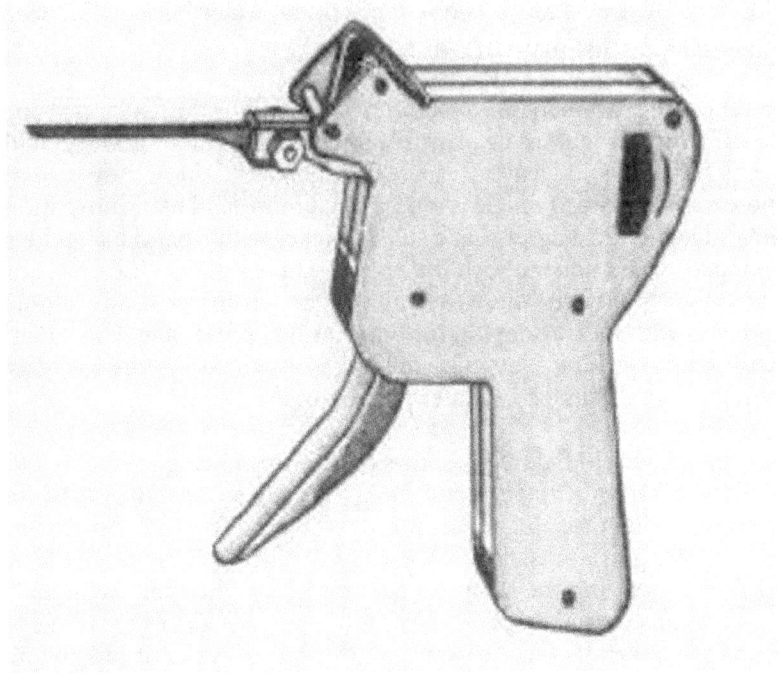

Fig 9.

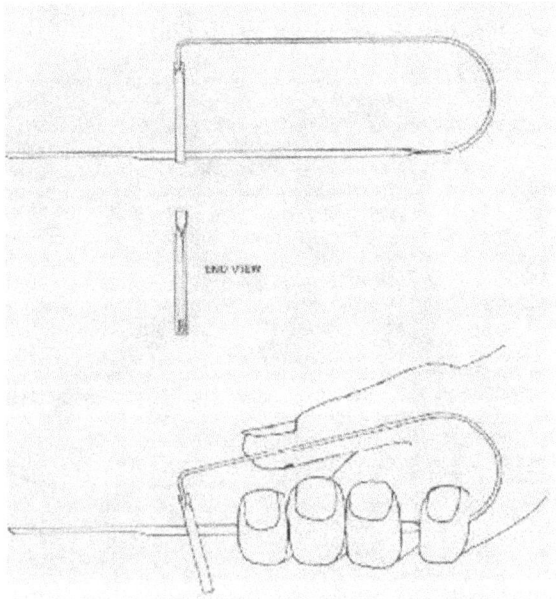

END VIEW

Fig 10.

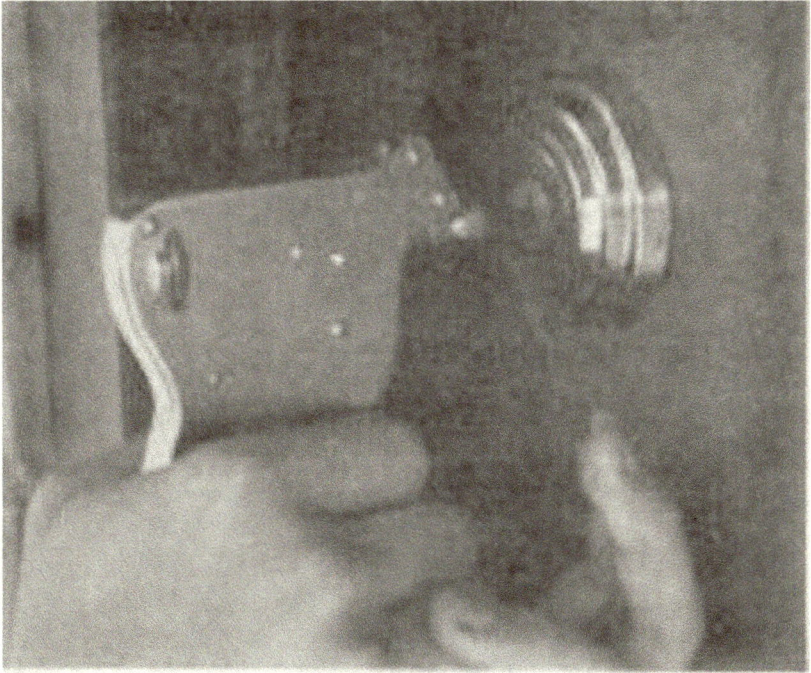

Fig 11.

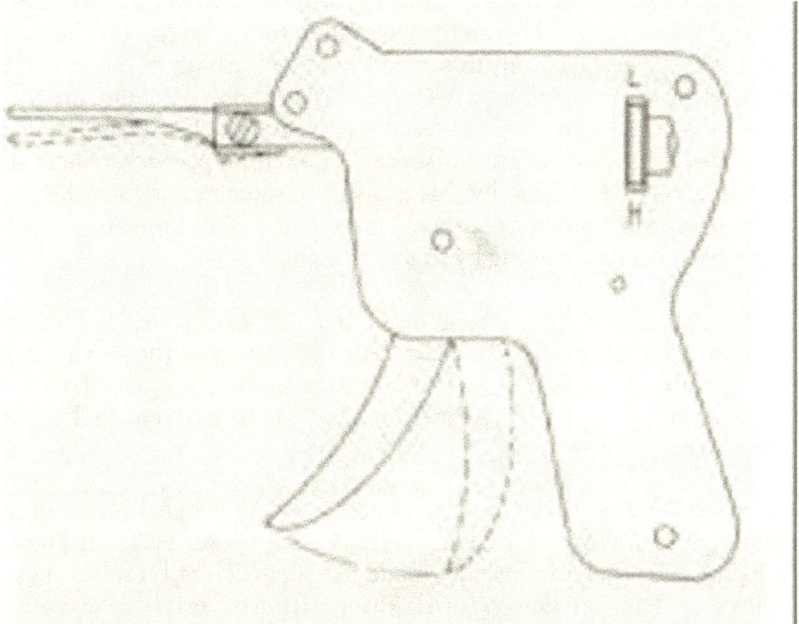

Fig 12.

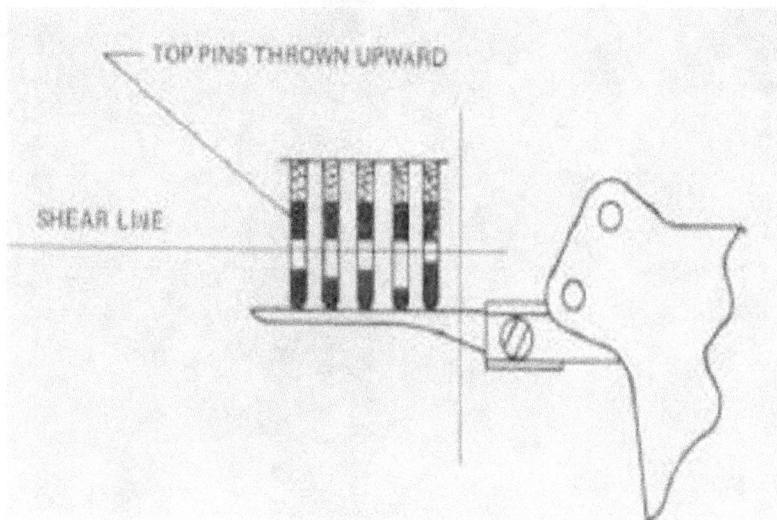

Fig 13.

Rapping - This subject is hardly worth mentioning, how- ever, since we are discussing, methods of causing all the pins to be thrown into a position whereby the plug can turn, we might touch, briefly, on the technique of "rapping". basically this entails striking the body of the lock with a plastic, rawhide or other protective hammer in the opposite direction than the pins have to travel to reach the shear line. This technique has been used with some degree of success in opening padlocks where the latch dog was acted upon by this transfer of force rather than the pins themselves. Most quality pad- locks have had design improvements to preclude to ease of opening by this technique.

Snapping, pick guns or rapping all make use of one well known law of physics known as Newton's law. For the benefit of those who slept through physics class this law briefly states that an object in motion or at rest will remain in that state until acted upon by another force.

Rocker Picks - This method is another rather hybrid method of opening a lock without the key. Some typical rocker picks are shown in Figure 15. These are usually made for a particular brand or type of lock as the random depth cuts must be fairly accurately spaced apart. The back side of the pick is ground to an oval; hence the name rocker pick. A typical set of these will have 10 or more different picks, the only difference being the different random cuts. The whole idea here is that with enough different cut combinations together with an applied rocking motion once the tool is inserted into the keyway, somewhere along the way all the pins will, by chance, be raised to the shear line at the same time.

Picks For Tubular Locks - The typical tubular lock has 7 pins located radically around a center post. This is considered to be a high security lock and is usually found in laundromat equipment, coin changers and vending machines. The picture in Figure 16 shows a commercially available pick tool for this type of lock. This tool departs from the techniques

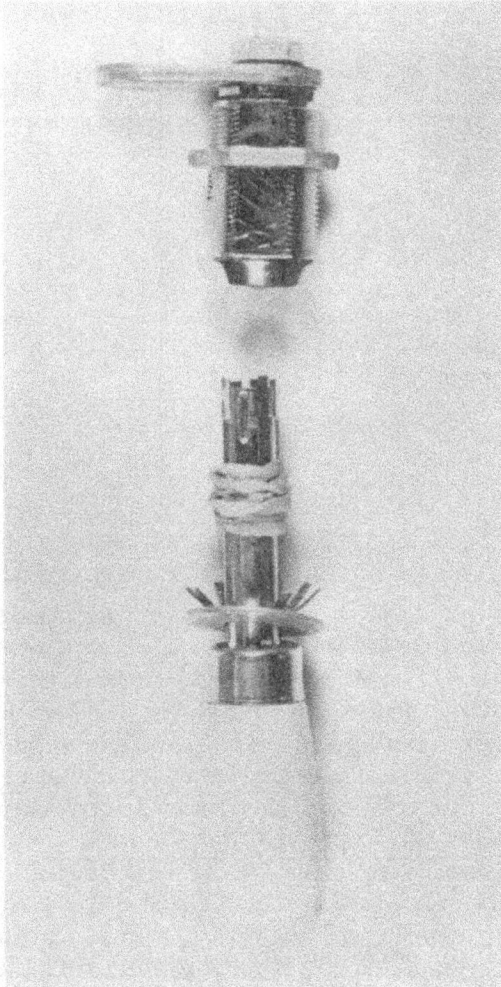

Fig 14.

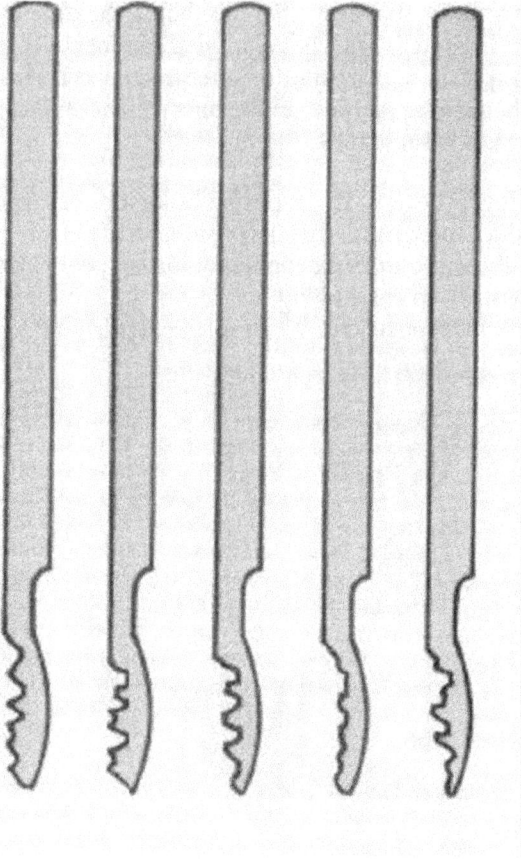

Fig 15.
and principles we have gone over thus far. This tool
imparts a turning torque also, and therefore a separate
torque wrench is not required. The tool actually impres-
sions more than it picks. It has 7 thin steel fingers that,
when a certain in & out motion is applied to the tool while
also applying a slight turning force, adjust themselves to
correspond to the cut depth of the key that would open
the lock. A rubber band or rubber sleeve provides friction
to hold the fingers semi-firmly in place. Once the lock opens
the fingers are held tighter by applying another rubber band
or tightening a rubber sleeve. When this is done the tool
can be used as a key to open the lock or as a guide to cut
a permanent key on a special key duplicating machine. The
picture in Figure 17 shows this tool in actual use.

Fig 16

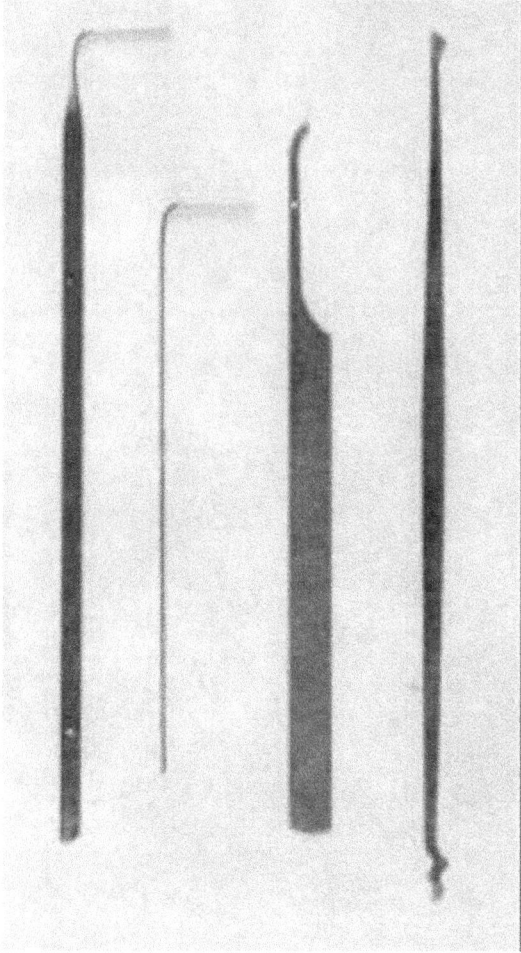

Fig 17.

COMMERCIALLY AVAILABLE PICKING TOOLS

Pick Sets - Almost as interesting as the evolution of locks is the evolution of lock picking tools (especially in the last few years). Archeological finds indicate lock picking tools have existed almost as long as locks themselves. In latter years professional pick sets for the locksmith trade ranged from two or three basic picks (which most professionals prefer) to a student set of six to ten picks. Now if you really want to impress your peers you can obtain a super deluxe set containing literally dozens of different picks, torsion wrenches, broken key extractors, etc., all contained in a genuine leather, double fold out, zipper closed case!!!

For years this was the way it was pick sets didn't increase in quality or useful design only in the number of picks and fancier cases to hold them. Tool manufacturers finally wised up and in the last few years have introduced smaller, better designed, and more practical sets than before.

When pick design stalemates, the manufacturers seem to concentrate on handle design or a novel way to package or contain the pick set. Pictured in Figure 18 you will see a basic set of two picks and a torsion wrench. This simple set will do about all a set with dozens of picks will do. Pictured in Figure 19 is a super fancy set for the elite picker. Pictured in Figures 20 and 21 you will see examples of better thought out and more practical pick sets. The trend to a different and exotic or novel way to package a pick set is shown in Figures 22 and 23. Here an attempt to present a "jack knife " type of toot set has been done. Actually this approach to pick set packaging is nothing new; the OSS (forerunner of the CIA), during WW II, designed a pick set contained in a real jack knife handle. Whether this was for convenience of concealment we are not quite sure. Some locksmiths have taken a regular pocket knife and ground picks from the blades. This is a questionable approach as the blades are made from hard and fairly brittle steel, they break too easily.

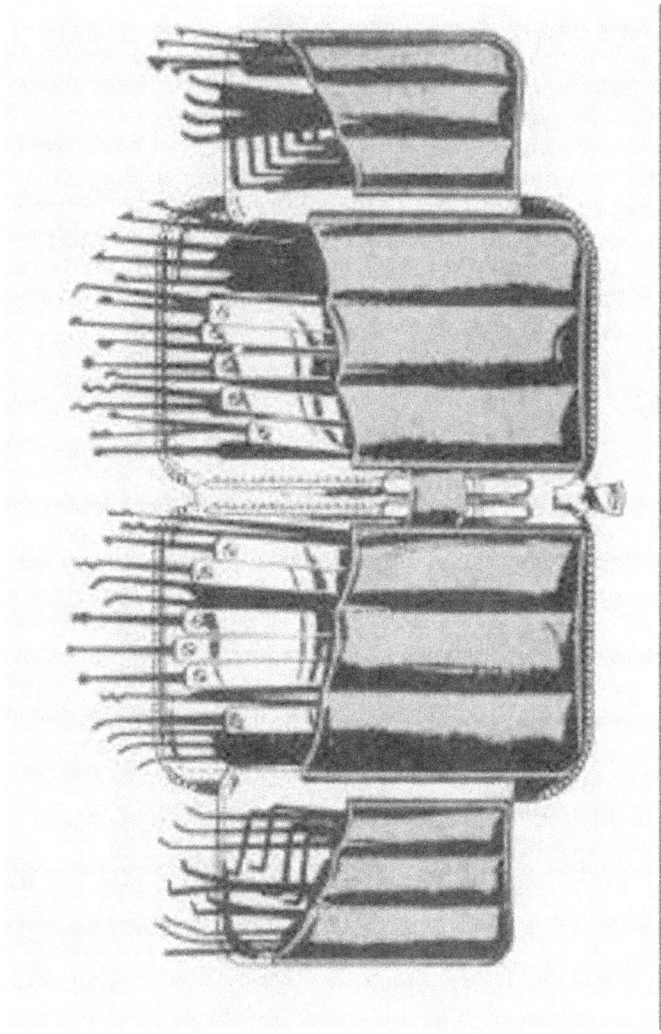

Fig 18.

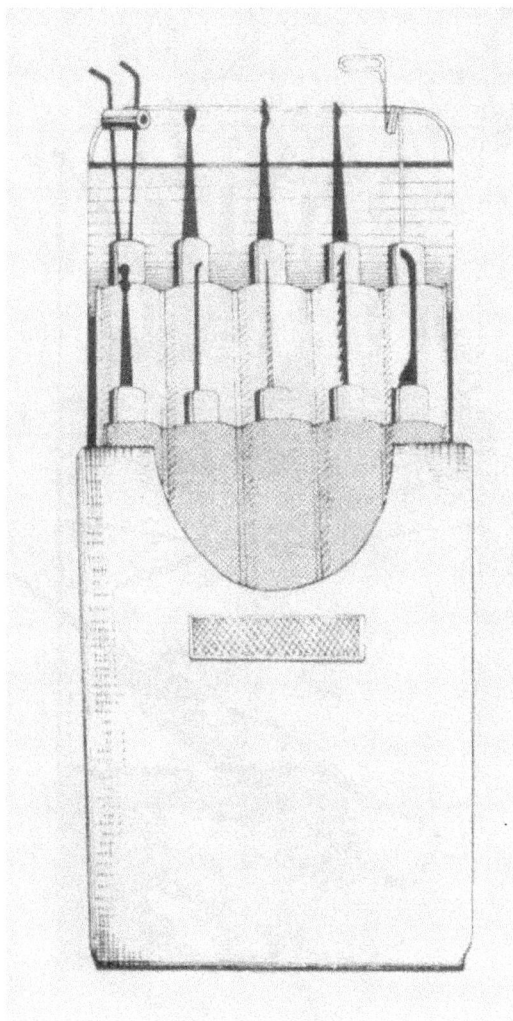

Fig 19,

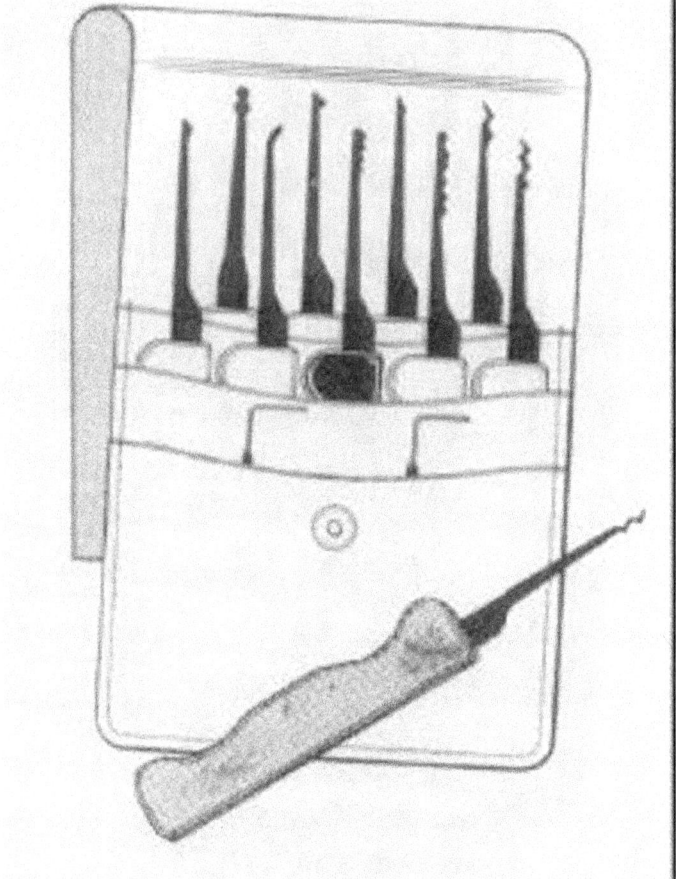

Fig 20.

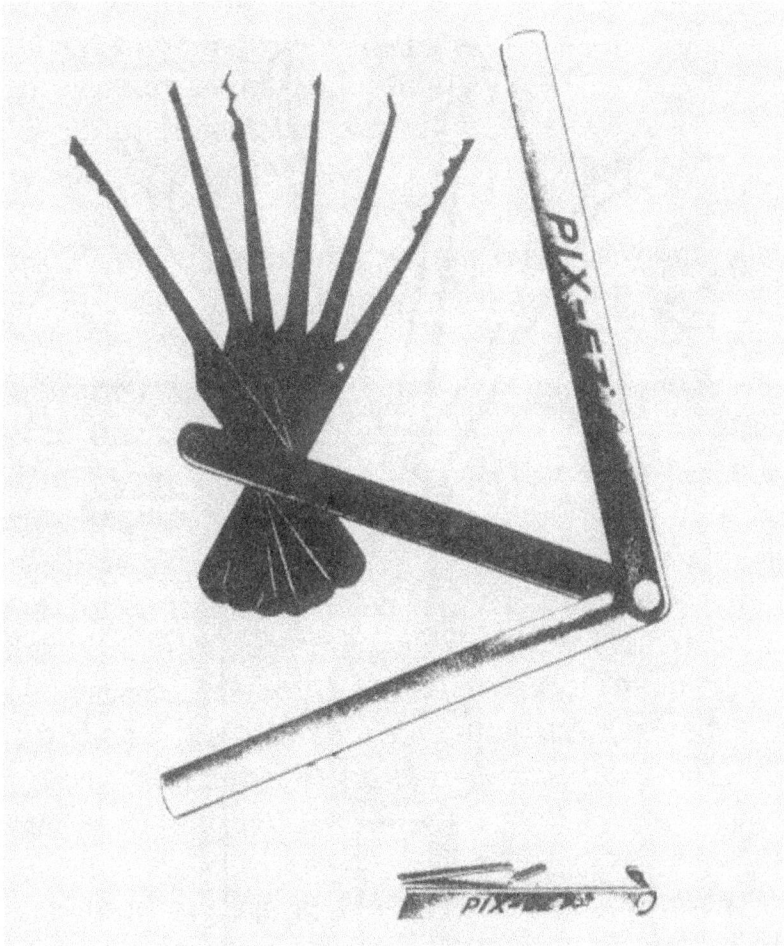

Fig 21

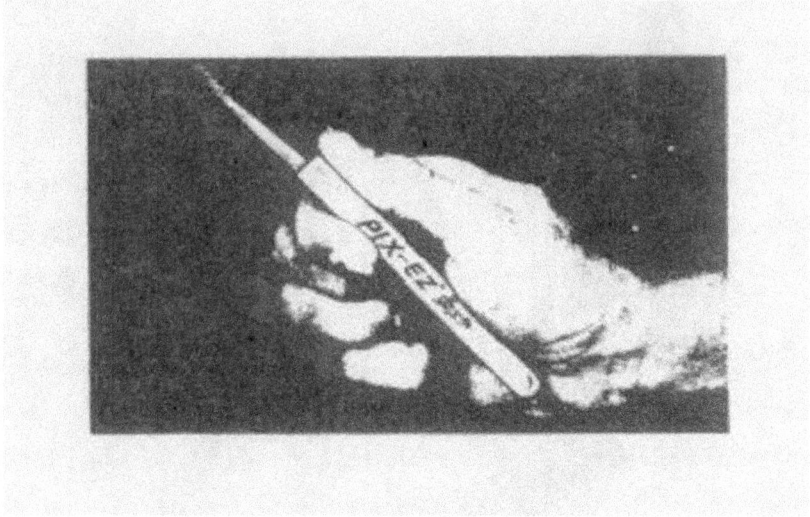

Fig 22.

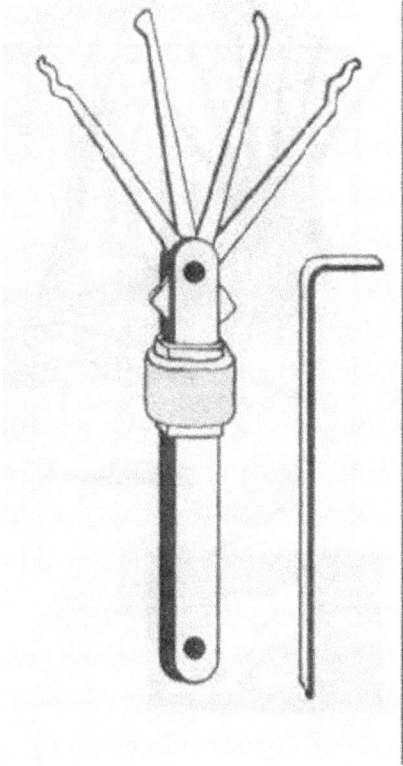

Fig 23.

Yet another approach to this problem is to break or grind off all the regular blade except for about 1/4 in. then silver solder a more conventional pick to the stub thus making a slightly more usable jack knife pick set. Since a torsion wrench is an indispensable part of a pick set, it must be carried separately from the knife.

In any case it is refreshing to see manufacturers take a fresh (or at least different) approach to pick set design.

Perhaps the most innovative pick set-design to come along recently is the pick set designed into a fountain pen as pictured in Figure 24. Figure 25 shows this same pen taken apart, revealing its "innards". Called a "007" pick set it contains 2 each of 3 basic pick styles: diamond, rake, and feeler. The need for a torsion wrench was cleverly answered by using the clip, which in this case is removable making a less than perfect, however, usable wrench. The picture in Figure 26 shows this pen tool in actual use. Carried in the pocket, along with other pens and pencils, this "007" pick set appears as an innocent felt tip pen.

One method of picking and type of lock we haven't yet discussed is the double sided lock. This type of lock is found on storage cabinets, desks and other medium security applications. Several years ago they were found on some vending machines. However, the tubular lock has now all but totally replaced them. Do not confuse the locks and keys used on Ford automobiles with double sided locks. The Ford lock is single sided - only the key is double sided, the purpose being that it can be inserted either way.

The picture in Figure 27 shows a typical double sided lock disassembled. Typically, these locks are of disc tumbler construction. You can see how these spring loaded wafers protrude from the plug. Installed into the housing, these wafers prevent the plug from turning.

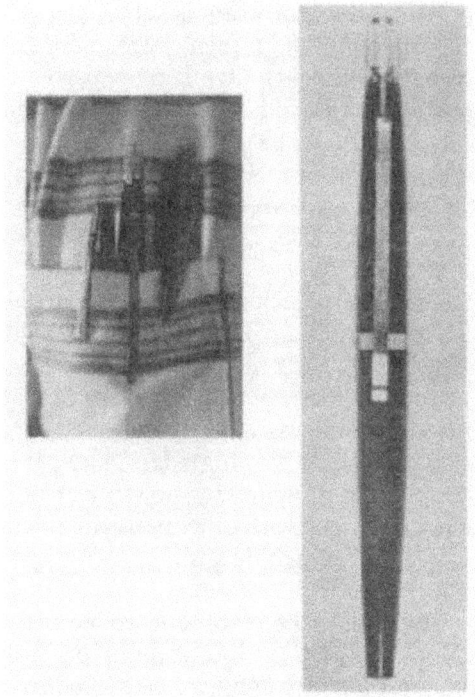

Fig 24.

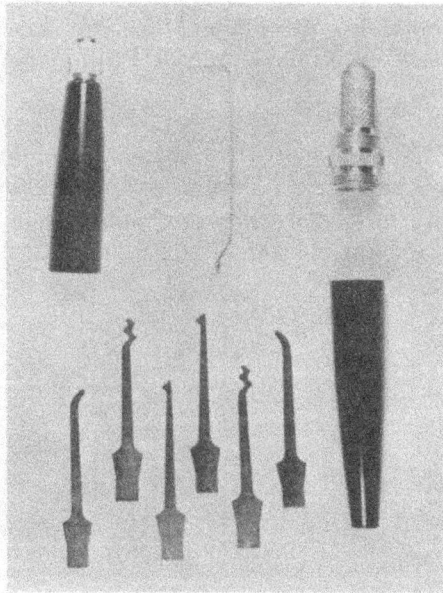

Fig 25.

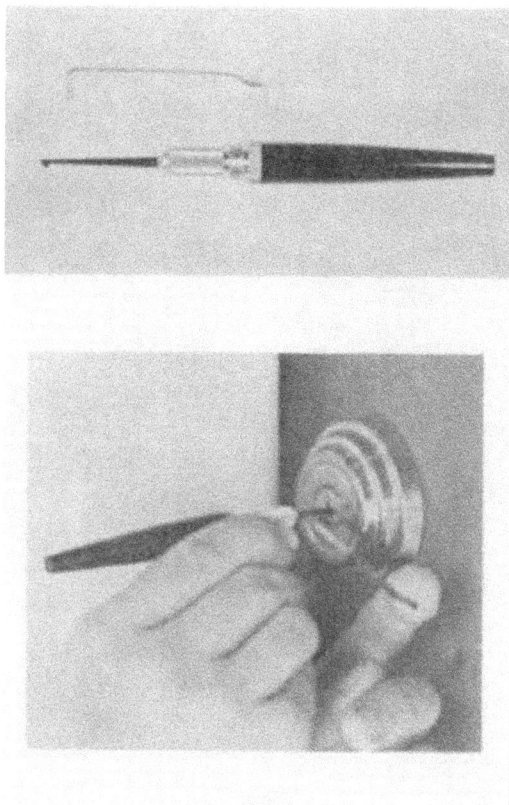

Fig 26.

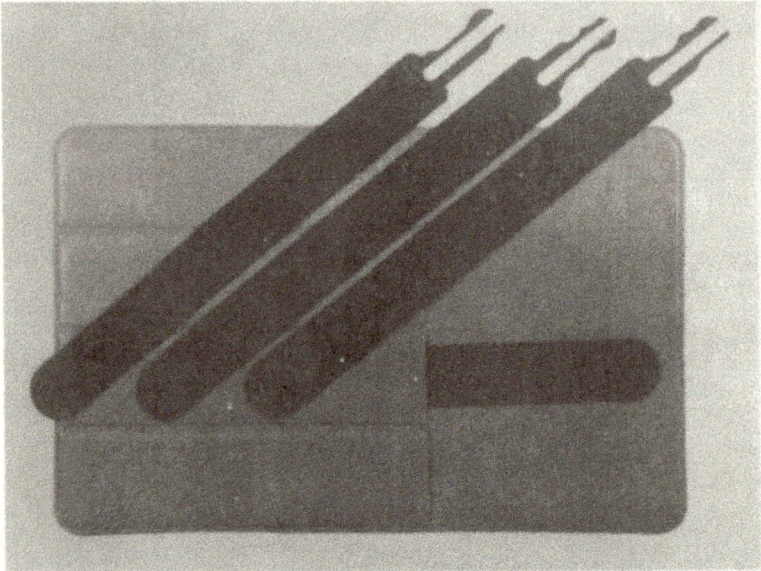

Fig. 27

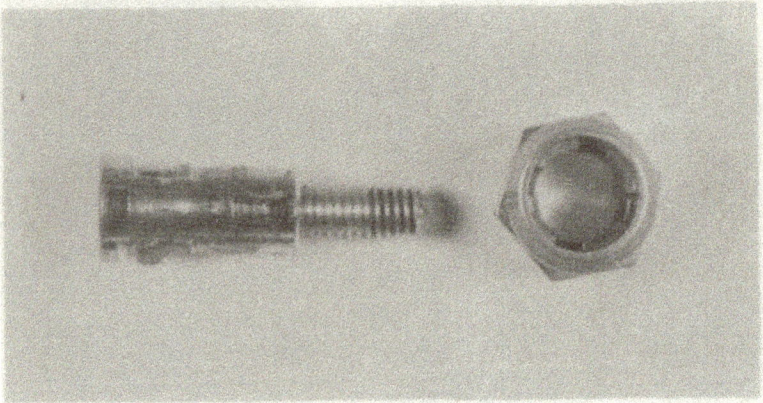

The picture in Figure 27 shows a set of commercially available double sided picks. Technically, these are a combination of a rake, a rocker pick and a try out key. The different tumbler cuts together with an up and down rocking motion will usually result in one of these picks opening the lock.

The picture in Figure 28 shows such a pick inserted into the plug previously shown. We can see that the tumblers are pulled back into the plug enough to let it rotate if it were in the housing. The fingers of these picks are slim, of hardened steel, and are easily broken if care is not exercised while applying the up and down motion.

\

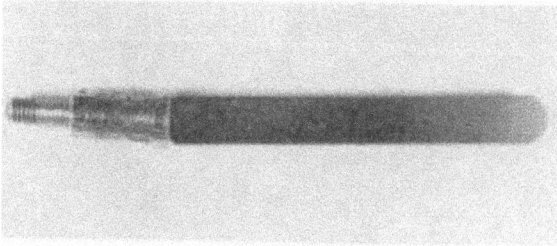

Fig 28

Schlage Wafer Picks - Pictured in Figure 29 is a unique set of picking tools. These are made specifically for picking the Schlage wafer tumbler lock. The set consists of two pairs of modified keys and two picks. These are pictured together with a pair of regular keys for comparison. These two pairs of modified keys are necessary because of Schlage's two different keyways and key tip configuration.

The drawing in Figure 30 shows the configuration in which this tool is used. The modified key provides a picking function, and also provides torque to facilitate the picking.

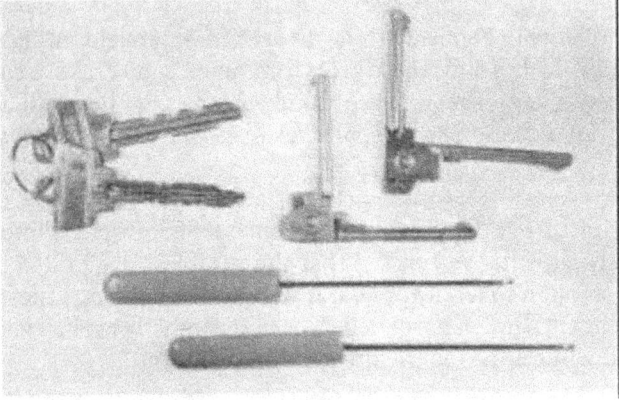

Fig 29

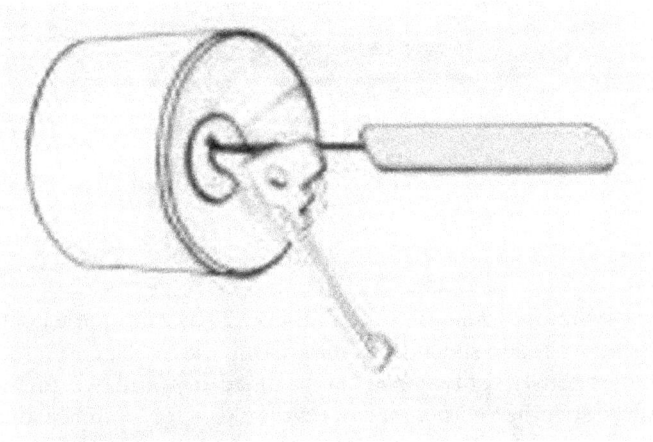

Fig 30

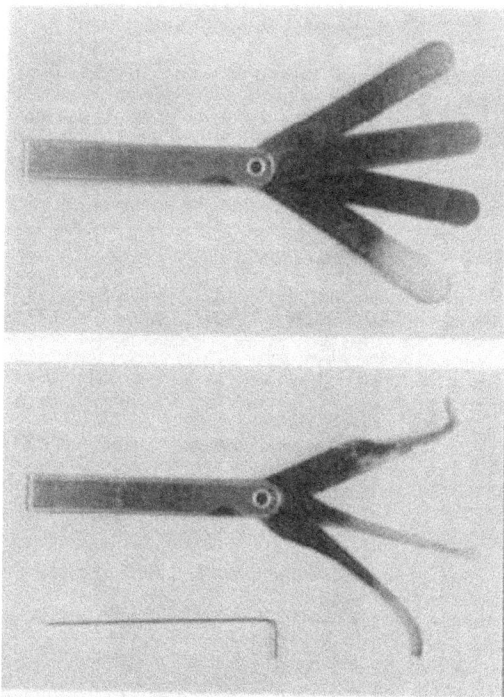

Fig 31.

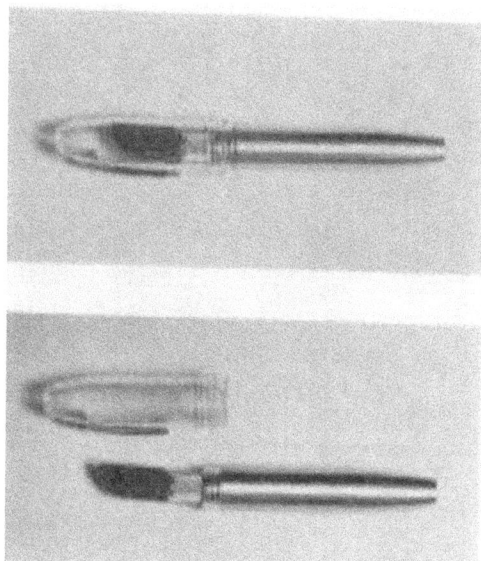

Fig 32.

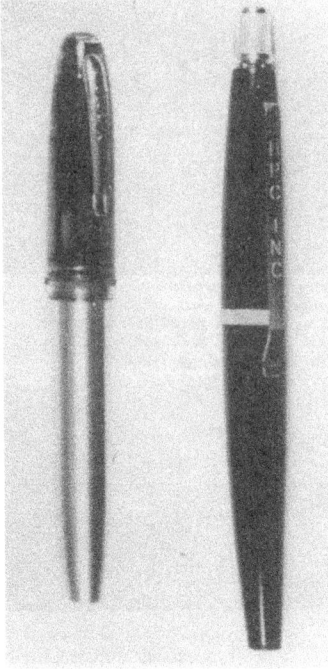

Fig 33.

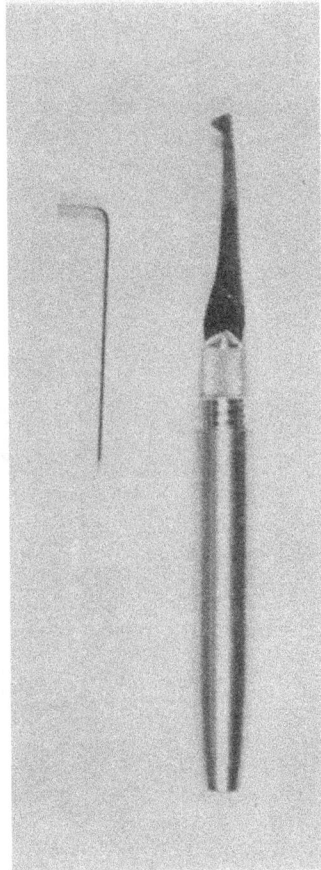

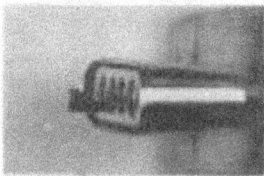

Fig 34.

Fig 35.

IMPROVISED PICKING TOOLS

Today there are literally hundreds of commercially available tools for the locksmith. Most of these tools started out as homemade versions and many of the commercially available tools around today can be, and have been duplicated by those handy with hand and machine. Only a few locksmithing tools require expensive or precision manufacturing machinery and processes. Most picks can be made by bending and grinding pieces of steel wire and flat steel spring material.

Any flat spring material ranging in thickness from .015 to .035 can he fashioned into a pick with the aid of a small grinder. One of the most common sources of such material is an automotive feeler gauge. These gauges have blades ranging in thickness from .001 to approximately .040 of an inch.

The picture in Figure 31 shows an improvised "jack knife" pick set which was made from an automotive feeler gauge. There are enough blades in a set like this to allow hand making a complete set of special and custom picking tools and shims.

One of the most original improvised pick sets to show up is pictured in Figure 34. This "007" type device was built around a readily available hobby knife. A similar knife, before modification is shown in Figure 35. The hollow handle is normally pressed on to the aluminum collet. On the improvised pick set this hollow has been altered to provide a slip fit, allowing it to be readily removed for access to its contents which happen to be a custom pick set together with a small torsion wrench. The clear plastic cap was painted black on the inside. This little jewel turns out to be more incognito than any commercially available set around today.

Picking the Sesame Padlock - This popular type padlock is shown in the picture in Figure 36. It has four combination wheels each being numbered from 0 to 9. The most unique feature of this padlock is that the combination numbers can be changed easily. This is accomplished while the lock is open by inserting a special tool into the open shackle hole and resetting the wheels to any desired new number.

Internally, these wheels have a changeable hub which has a flat spot on it. When these four flat spots are aligned together toward the side of the lock having the trademark stamped on it, the remaining mechanism can move so as to unlock the shackle.

Also pictured in Figure 36 is an improvised picking tool for this lock. Actually this tool does not pick the lock but aids us in determining an unknown combination number. The picture in Figure 37 shows this tool inserted into the lock. Being made from .005 shim stock, it slips between the wheel and housing. In the position shown it is used to feel for the flat spot as the wheel is turned. Once the flat spots are found, 5 is either added or subtracted from the indicated number to have the correct combination number.

HANDCUFFS

A book on lock picking for police would not be complete without a brief look at handcuffs. This is one locking device that is close to daily activities of almost every law enforcement officer. Every officer should be familiar with the locking mechanism, especially how easily handcuffs can be picked open.

With the exception of a few low cost imports, there are two popular brands of handcuffs used in the United States. These are the Peerless and the Smith & Wesson. These are almost identical in design and construction. Both have a double lock feature for the benefit of both the cuffer and the cuffee. On double locks, the jaw cannot be closed any tighter, thus cutting off the circulation and also cannot be shimmed open with a bobby pin.

The picture in Figure 36 shows a pair of Smith & Wesson Model 90 handcuffs together with keys. The keyways can be seen. The keys are small hollow bit keys with a pin-like protrusion extending from the bow (handle).

The picture in Figure 37 shows the double lock plunger hole that is on the side of the frame on both cuffs. The double lock feature is activated by pressing the pin on the key into this hole. The double lock is unlocked by inserting the key into the keyway and turning the opposite direction than when just unlocking the jaw.

Because of their small profile and light weight design, handcuffs have the simplest of lock mechanisms. While these locks are strong and are generally secure enough for their application, a law enforcement officer should be aware just how easy they are to open. The picture in Figure 40 shows these cuffs being shimmed open with a thin piece of steel. Over the years, bobby pins have become just about the standard tool for this operation, probably because of their presence almost everywhere including the crack in the rear seat of your patrol car. When was the last time you checked this before taking a car out?

The pictures in Figures 38 and 39 show a ball point pen's Insides and the cuffs being opened by a key fashioned from this pen. In this particular case, the inside of the ball point pen was transformed into a handcuff key in about five seconds with the only tool being a nail clipper. With a little more time and effort a much better improvised key could be made.

We hope that these two simple illustrations have made he point of how important it is to keep even the simplest of raw materials away from the dexterous cuffee.

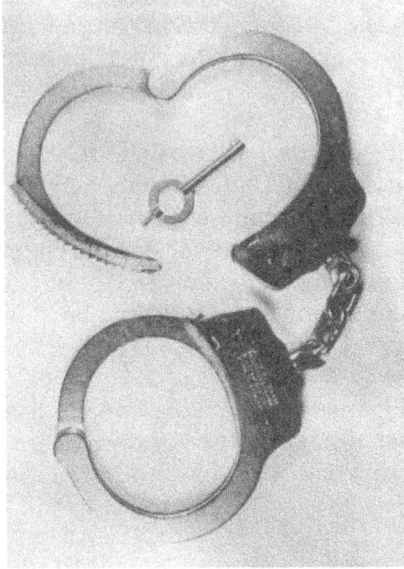

Fig 36.

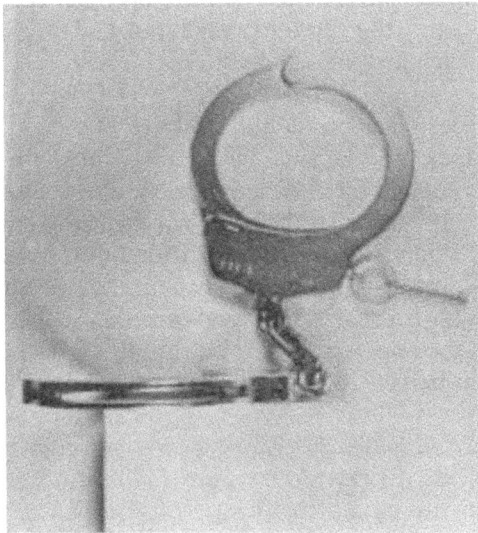

Fig 37.

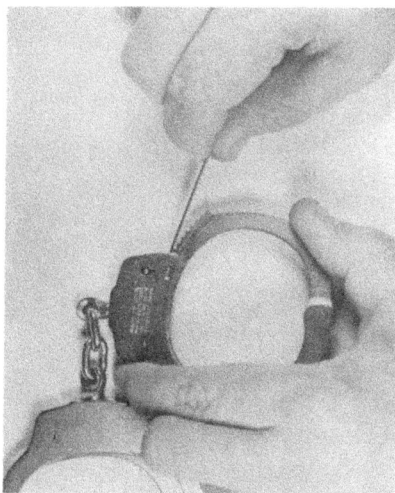

Fig 38.

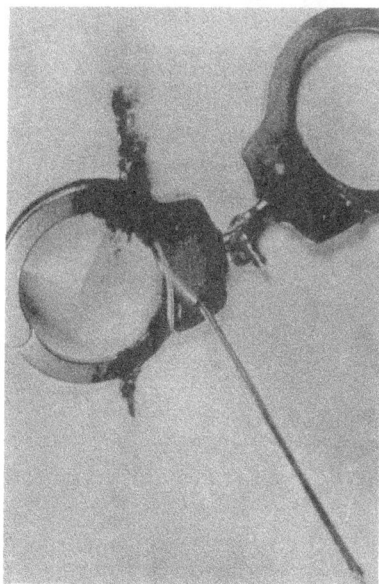

Fig 39.

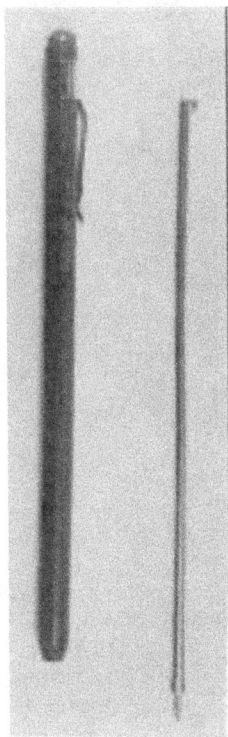

CONCLUSION

You, the reader, have just seen most of the inner secrets of lock picking. We have looked briefly at some of the more common types of locks and the established ways of picking each one.

While the tools used differ, the basic ingredients of skill and dexterity remain the same. Lock picking is not easy. You may "luck out" sometimes but will usually spend several minutes, sometimes hours before succeeding. No lock picking tool will perform by itself any more than an artists paint brush.

Lock picking is hardly a skill of the fence hopping, run of the mill burglar. He seldom has the knowledge or patience. These operators usually find enough open windows and unlocked doors to satisfy their needs.

Lock picking enters the larcenous arena when the stakes are high. These stakes are usually items of high monetary value when burglary is concerned or intelligence gathering where espionage is involved. It is only here where the high security and "pick resistant" locks are really worth their extra cost and only then when combined into an overall physical security system.

For the average home owner the extra security afforded by pick resistant locks should be added only after tending to more vulnerable points of security on their premises.

With little or no expenditure, existing locks can be made more secure by ascertaining that there is enough difference in the cuts on the key so as not to allow a knife blade or similar straight instrument to lift the tumblers to the shear line. It is also good practice to eliminate master keying found in most tract homes. Recently purchased or rented homes should be rekeyed by the new occupant. You can never be sure just who the former owner or occupant gave keys to.

In "pick resistant" lock design, attention is usually focused on the pins. The "mushroom" pin was one of the first attempts to foil regular picking techniques. Here the top pin, rather than being a straight, smooth sided pin is machined to appear as a small, mushroom shaped spool. If you are now familiar with basic pin tumbler design, you can readily see how these work.

All in all there needs to be more attention to complete home security rather than concentrate on a "pick proof" lock or cylinder. The extra cost of this lock might be better spent in other areas of physical security. This does not mean such a lock won't enhance an already good system, only that it should be considered in the proper perspective.